Shakti Morgane's

Book of Shadows

A Guide to Soul Salvation

Shakti Morgane's

Book of Shadows

I summon the Great Goddess,

in the form of the mighty Three.

Take away the evil

and make me free.

Help me now and make it flee.

As I will it. So mote it be.

***

Evil gives way to the one who has the sun in his heart. (Isis, ancient Egyptian goddess)

Book of Shadows

© 2019 Christiane Hausmann
Author: Shakti Morgane (Pseudonym)
Manufacture and publishing: Books on Demand GmbH,
Norderstedt
ISBN: 9783753472584
2021

Cover image by Manfred Antranias Zimmer, Pixabay;
Figure on p. 17 by Peter Lomas,Pixabay; p. 18:
Educational Centre Tai Ji Quan; p. 39   Esther
Casla; p. 46   OpenClipart-Vectors, Pixabay; p. 23
John Hain, Pixabay; p. 27   Aline Ponce, Pixabay; p.
51 a. p. 97 Clker-Free-Vector-Images, Pixabay
Translated from german into english with
www.DeepL.com/Translator (free version)

Table of contents

Feminine strength and spiritual nature power

It is female nature to connect with the vibrations and elements in the world and within herself to bring forth, protect, nurture and sustain new life. This ability became increasingly fatal to women when it was no longer needed for immediate survival. The special ability of the female part of humanity to communicate with nature and to bring about change by means of psychic power was forgotten throughout history as essential for survival and was understood less and less, even by women themselves. In the period from about the 14th to the 18th century, this ability was increasingly demonised in Europe and denigrated as being 'in league with the devil', and used as a pretext to scapegoat and exterminate about 1 million people, especially women, by means of the Inquisition.

Only in modern times, thanks to the fact that an enlightened culture of knowledge has been established, is one again able to demystify human nature and put both religious and ideological delusion in its place.

In tradition, literature and art, there is evidence of the partly successful handling of various psychological states into which man can fall when it comes to warding off 'evil' events in order to shape his life.

However, modern man is generally characterised by a lack of strength of soul or personal power (psych.: 'dependent personality disorder') in the face of adversity in life. Moreover, nowadays envy of the female potency of childbearing produces a postmodern form of 'witch-hunt': *the aim is to abolish women as mothers as far as possible in order to replace nature with the artificial creation of patriarchal science.* (von Werlhof)

Therefore, in the age of technical progress, the rise of modern man's longing for the lost abilities to communicate with nature - an ability that promises great soul power - can be increasingly observed.

An inkling of such spiritual power is conveyed by the well-known novel by M. Bulgakov published in the 20th century: "The Master and Margarita".

In this novel, Bulgakov addresses the contradiction between determinism and voluntarism in the Soviet Union of the Stalin era. His solution to the problem: the occult! The 'devil' fetches the technocrats! Because the moral of the story here is: those who manage to overcome their fear and thus transform their pain into relaxation, like Margarita, contribute to chaos breaking into the world of their adversaries from behind the scenes. Thus, for the purpose of strengthening the soul in the face of adversity, it is a matter of emotional transformation! The 'spirits' that create chaos in Margarita's adversaries have crossed over into reality from a parallel universe to come to Margarita's aid. They have been summoned by Margarita's ability for emotional transformation.

Magic is an independent energy. It is available to each of us and is activated through emotional transformation. The basic prerequisite for this is the ability to relax. Then magic becomes an active force. Relaxation, in turn, means releasing a problem from the mind, to get to the bottom of such emotions as anger, fear, delusion, and so on, - the shadows! Each of us can strengthen our soul by purifying the 'heart' (self-knowledge!) and thereby use powers from the underworld to solve our problems.

The 'Book of Shadows' helps to remember which spiritual tools have helped in dissolving 'shadows' (Jung) and which magical actions have been crowned with success.

Balance

Unnoticed fears, undiscovered manipulations, negative emotions and thoughts - the shadows - make you ill in the long run. Illness is an imbalance in spiritual terms, is one-sidedness in relation to the power that balances.

Illness is a drive conflict (e.g. between sexual drive and food drive) because of personal imbalances due to entanglements.

By means of illness, our body, the obedient servant of our soul, reminds us that we have a soul to which we should finally listen.

But one can also accept suffering as personal fate, according to the motto: dying is part of life, nothing can be done about it.

But that is not the same as:

'Especially today, don't worry, don't be angry, be grateful, be kind, take care of your circumstances'. (Usui)

In this case you have to actively seek and find balance by taking care of your own circumstances.

Life is balance, equilibrium. If someone is ill, he has lost his centre.

The balancing of the vibrations can take place through movement, in which we integrate and balance above and below, right and left, front and back, inside and outside, e.g. in dance. The body makes the movement and the soul follows.

A soul is a being of light. The divine spark within us. The soul acts according to its own rules, those of the Ma'at (great goddess), and protests against the character if it moves too far away from the Ma'at. The body reacts with indisposition, even illness. That is why, in this case, shamans want to bring back the soul.

A shaman is a seer. A shaman has a guardian spirit. From him he gets strength.

The shaman proves himself in different states of consciousness. The shaman is a distributor of power. It is about spiritual power.

Soul retrieval is protective spirit retrieval or power animal retrieval.

When someone became despondent, the shaman would travel to the underworld and retrieve the power animal. The retrieved guardian spirit (power animal) is first blown into the chest, then into the fontanel on the patient's head.' (Harner)

The 'other side' (Silva) / otherworld from which the shaman retrieves the guardian spirit (soul) is the underworld / astral world and the frustration /

emotion is at the same time the fuel to transform the emotion. But one can also change the body frequency oneself and e.g. go into the alpha state (trance) and ask the Higher Self, the immortal part of the Self, to transform the frustration into something else, such as wish fulfilment / need satisfaction. This works in every case. When frustrated, always seek one's own centre / relaxation, this includes at the same time:

- the balance

- reciprocity

- overcoming the inner resistance caused by

  one-sidedness

- the 'impeccability' (Castaneda)

'Vampire' / Energy Predator

When someone in a family is very ill, there is often a case of energy vampirism (emotional abuse). For example, all those suffering from abandonment become energy vampires. One 'vampire' (narcissist) creates the other 'vampire'. Anyone who has been sucked by a 'vampire' becomes a 'vampire' themselves.

'Vampires' are in perpetual search of love due to abandonment trauma in childhood and / or past lives. However, they are incapable of love. They suck others dry because they only use them to quench their thirst. They cannot give anything themselves because they have not received love. 'Vampires' are insolent. They steal the life force of others.

Addiction comes from wasting away, wasting away because of vampirism. The addict wants to run away from himself, he wants to run away from his pain. Without drugs, this becomes depression. Something pulls the addict into the beyond, he has to look at that. An addict has developed the pain avoidance strategy of putting himself on the sidelines or outside the group. The group is too painful for him because of its vampirism and cannot be endured without drugs.

To be bored means to have a 'vampire' on your hands. To be bored means to waste your time, your life time.

According to Dufour, the only way to escape the feeling of tension that results from boredom is to focus on the body in the 'here and now' and to switch off the 'thinking', to let the chattering mind rest. *But when the mind rests, there is no time and therefore no time to waste through boredom.* (Buddha)

'To let the mind rest' means to meditate. To meditate is to stop the carousel of thoughts.

Meditation is the school of the mind. Through 'mind' you change your body vibration. You have to change your body vibration when you feel uncomfortable. It is about transforming a low frequency into a high frequency. Buddha nature is a certain high body vibration.

You go into the alpha state and concentrate on colour, light, or invoke the divine vibration by feeling into the movement of belly dancing, or concentrate on a symbol, or recite a mantra, until you are calm and relaxed. That is quite enough.

Therefore, for the purpose of transforming vibration, always meditate when you feel unwell.

The transformation of negativity (darkening of the mind / shadow) is necessary because negativity sooner or later drives us to death, because *'energy follows attention'* (Kahili King).

The best means of transmutation for shadows that I know is belly dancing in combination with meditation, because this dance comes from a time when life was celebrated and worshipped (fertility cult / the 'Old Path'), while meditation trains the mind. The transformation of shadows, when one dances, is done by the spirit through the body by changing the frequency of the body into the vibration corresponding to one's own spirit. For this purpose, one must know the vibration (music) corresponding to one's own spirit. The multitude of rhythms and movement combinations of oriental dance, which have been handed down for thousands of years, provide the appropriate vibration for each spirit and thus guarantee again the change of the body vibration in the direction of life / joy.

Suddenly fat

The sickness of our time is meaninglessness (ignorance!).

Resulting emotions / frustrations / shadows that are not perceived lead to 'frustration eating' and make people fat. The fat person tries to eat away 'inner emptiness'.

The hero in the TV film *"Plötzlich fett!"* (SAT.1, 2011) had to learn that the fat woman obviously has power over him, recognise her importance and act accordingly.

Conclusion of the TV film: You cannot ignore others if they have power over you.

Why do they have power over you? Because we are all connected in the unconscious / underworld, on the energy level!

If you are being ignored, then you must demonstrate your power. You must not 'sit' on your negative emotions / shadows. Transformation of negative emotions: this is best done with a curse, as suggested in the film above, or through dance and meditation (concentration), or lucid dreaming. Lucid dreaming is when you consciously do things in your dreams that cannot be done in waking life.

Lucid dreaming

The underworld or astral world is an existing medium into which one passes during sleep. The soul is wandering in another dimension. This dimension is not strictly separated from the waking reality. During sleep, the consciousness of the person continues to exist in another frequency (brain waves). Dimensions differ in the frequencies of their vibrations. Access to another dimension is gained through a different body vibration. Through meditation, one changes the body vibration. Buddhist monks have been doing this for thousands of years. They change their body vibration until the body begins to float, for example. Meditation is the concentration of thoughts on a focus, e.g. light, colour, symbol, imagination, mantra, breathing, movement, and so on. Apparently, in meditation one can tune into a wave by means of concentration, in which emotions / shadows change.

Three forces govern the universe: Shiva, Vishnu and Brahma (the destroyer, the creator and the preserver / balancer) or in ancient Egyptian terms: Hathor, Ra and Ma'at, all of which are one and the same - the All-One. When an imbalance occurs between two forces and one force prevails, the third one 'steps in' and provides balance again. On the earthly level in social relationships, however, this does not happen automatically. The balance only occurs when the third force is perceived.

Tiredness is a kind of trance when one is on the wrong path, has no relation to reality. Inner fire (feeling of warmth) one has, *'when the soul is in the realm where the spirit of truth and life communicates with it every day, then you transform the difficulties on the earthly plane'*. (Cayce)

The fourth dimension is the subtle / astral plane, the effect plane, the underworld, the penetrating and the connecting.

The etheric body of the human being transports the will / spirit. The higher the vibration of the etheric body, the more effective the human being. The will is part of the underworld / astral world.

The spirit brings things about by the soul doing them in conscious (lucid) dreaming.

For the purpose of lucid dreaming, you must be aware in the dream that you are dreaming. Begin the exercise by looking for your hands in the dream.

Gradually increase in this exercise until, while dreaming, you can see yourself in the dream.

If you dream your reality yourself, then prophetic dreams (clairvoyance) are expressions of your own creation, your real will, in the underworld / astral plane.

"Seeing" in Castaneda means: to see with the eyes of the soul. *There are no limits.* (Kahili King)

The 'Old Path'

In ancient times, nature was worshipped in the form of the Great Goddess.

In Greek mythology, *the goddess dances wildly in the darkness until Ophion, the great serpent, rises behind her. She seizes the great serpent, who mates with her. She becomes pregnant and gives birth to the light.* (von Ranke-Graves)

This scene illustrates how consciousness (*light*) is created, just as new life is created in the sexual act with the body moving into a rhythm.

In this scene, the snake represents the soul, and the soul communicates with us through our body. The Greek creation myth symbolises: when we tune into a rhythm with our body, we have the possibility to 'see' in the body. What is there to see? It is about the realisation of the soul's needs!

For those who consider the soul to be a 'divine spark', they communicate with their goddess / god / spirit via the body. Therefore, *for witches* (followers of the 'Old Path'*) dancing is a religious experience.* (Langwasser)

All injustices in the field of forces of social relations and imbalances in personal relations make the shadow emerge. The shadow is the visible separation of body and mind, is the displacement of the 'mounting point' (Castaneda).

Accordingly, all imbalances initiate the separation of body and mind and block the life energy, which can go as far as death (the final separation). Blocked life energy takes a form of stagnation, torpor, heaviness, total darkness. But the Goddess rules the darkness. Just as, according to the law of the Goddess, light regenerates itself in darkness, the spirit of man regenerates itself in the emotional world of the body, in the subconscious, in sleep, in dreams. Immersing oneself in the emotional world of the body through dreams, rhythm, meditation or by consulting the oracle makes it possible to see the interrelation of the forces behind things, so that one can then behave correctly, in harmony with one's own centre, with the balancing force (Ma'at). The right decision can be felt physically as lightness, relaxation or inner peace.

We worship in the Great Goddess the universal energy of life.

The manifesto of the Great Goddess honours the spiritual forces of nature and, according to my revelation, has the following content:

I am the great Goddess (the Tao, the Ma'at)
who created the universe. I am the ruler of
light and darkness.
Matter ('the devil')
with its opposites, cycles and conflicts
('demons')
is subject to me and your immortal soul
belongs to me.
Whenever you call upon me and ask for help, I
will assist you.
Therefore do not despair and go your way with
confidence.
For I am what was in the beginning and what
will be achieved in the end.

Matter with its opposites, cycles and conflicts:

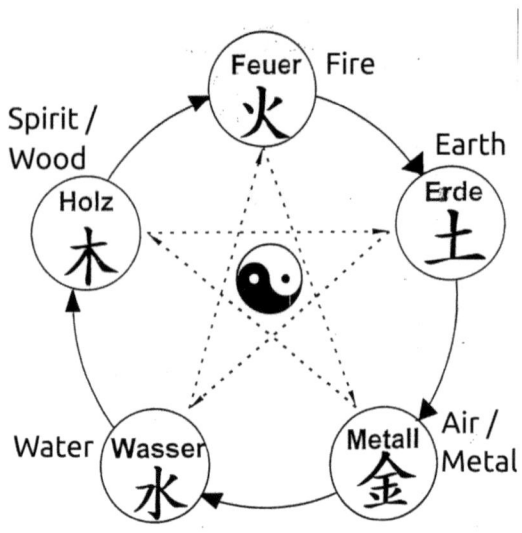

Feng Shui and Karma

Feng Shui also deals with the effect of the spiritual forces of nature in space and time in order to bring harmony into the connection between living space and time, dwelling and fate (karma). Your dwelling reflects your destiny. Destiny is what you make of the given circumstances. That in turn depends on your character. Your character is your destiny. The conditions of existence in the family into which we were born and to which we owe our lives have shaped our character, a psychic form or structure that can break along certain lines (fault lines, boundaries, blockages, shadows, black holes in the aura) as soon as a sufficiently strong force acts on it and as long as we are not able to use the respective counterforce to close the black holes / lighten the shadows.

The conditions of the family's existence are a product of culture and nowadays this culture is characterised by the fact that in the education of individuals, there is a separation between feeling and emotional awareness. Thus, we often no longer know what we ourselves want and cannot decide in our own interest. The unrecognised shadows in the subconscious then attract what is sent to us. In this respect, we create everything ourselves and can also change it ourselves by 'bringing the shadows into consciousness'.
Parents make mistakes in their upbringing because of their own trauma. Then there is the inherited destiny from the family clan, from the ancestors. Then there is the couple relationship: *'He who loves must share the fate of the one he loves'*. (Bulgakov) Accordingly, there are a lot of karmic traces to overcome before fate falls into place. We actively change fate / karma by changing our character. For example, one can learn to become more patient, or to set boundaries, or to overcome anger, and so on. In this learning phase, one has to face one's fears and other negative emotions in order to dissolve the karmic traces.
In Buddhism (Bön), negative emotions are confronted, for example, by means of dream yoga.
From the inside, by transforming emotions, and from the outside, e.g. with Feng Shui, one can bring about the change of fate / karma.
The usual concept of karma is a lifeless construct (sterile cause-effect chain). There is no karma if the actions are in harmony with the force that

balances or: if one calls the 'demon' by its name, one is free from karma / external determination.

Karma is the circumstances of life, the external determination. The usual concept of karma means: what you sow you reap. For example, if you want to experience love, you have to give love, says the principle of sowing and reaping. Is that true? Not necessarily!

Karma is external determination. If you want to experience love, you have to recognise foreign determination, manipulation. Because karma is in any case foreign determination in the 'here and now'. Karma purification takes place through the recognition of foreign determination or life circumstances.

The social relationships of the human being are regulated in the unconscious by the *'orders of love/soul'* (Hellinger). *There is no body-soul unity.* (Plack) What Freud did not know: if one violates these orders of the soul, e.g. in education, this leads to frustrations and drive conflicts in the individual. Then people can be directed or manipulated on the basis of their unsatisfied needs, e.g. by means of advertising and propaganda.

How can you escape this black magic? By becoming aware of one's own spiritual needs. To do this, one must first become aware of one's own needs. *,It is helpful to have a method or process that allows you to explore the depths of your unconscious'.* (Sagan) Hellinger uses the method of family constellations for this purpose.

In addition, physical exercises such as belly dancing, yoga, tai chi, qigong, and meditation also help. In this way one lifts the mood (body frequency). Bad moods associated with frustrations disappear and the black magicians no longer have power.

Remember: No one consumes useless stuff or goes to war who is happy and content. Unless he goes to war to learn to fear. (Folk saying: When the donkey gets too comfortable, he goes on the ice.) One escapes the doom (karma) only if one completely frees oneself from emotions such as greed, fear and anger.

Since time immemorial, the search for peace of mind (Nirvana) has been at the centre of ancient religions and Asian worldviews.

In Taoism, it is assumed that it is forces that shape the world and whose vibrations can be brought into harmony to attract happiness.

This results in people playing an active role in shaping their destiny / character. In Feng Shui, this leads to 8 tasks of self-creation or spiritualisation and regeneration according to the 8 cardinal points of the earth.

Since Mother Earth provides us with the spiritual forces of nature in addition to the material ones, we have the possibility to make use of a large number of aids when dealing with the inner and outer forces that affect us.

Precious and semi-precious stones, whose vibrations work in the energy body and can help us in our tasks by strengthening our own psychic power, have proven their worth.

Feng Shui names, for example, the **Northwest**, which symbolises Helpful People, Friends, Mentors. Should there be a toilet, kitchen, storage room, a missing or additional area in the NW of our home, we could have a problem, depending on and in combination with our personal Feng Shui, because the NW does not fit harmoniously into the floor plan of our home and / or is only available to us in a limited way. In this case, friends, mentors, benevolent superiors may be missing. Perhaps even the father was not present or was not supportive in the upbringing. This may have resulted in a difficult psychological situation and we may now be faced with the task of conquering fears and depression. In addition to Feng Shui measures for the home, which I cannot go into here due to lack of space, there are also helpful stones for coping with this task in meditation, including, for example: clear crystal quartz, cat's eye, tiger iron, amber.

Clear crystal quartz heals us by transporting divine light into our soul and aura.
Cat's eye gives warmth and security.
Tiger iron works against exhaustion and brings new energy.
Amber promotes encounters with people who take us further.

The **north** symbolises career. If there is a toilet, kitchen, storage room, a missing or additional area in the N of our home, we could have a problem, depending on and in combination with our personal Feng Shui, because the N does not fit harmoniously into the floor plan of our home and / or is only available to us in a limited way. Then there may be a lack of a straight path up the career ladder, because one encounters obstacles in advancing professionally. Maybe we only ever find part-time jobs or low-paid jobs, or we are bullied and so on. In the long run, you feel 'small' and not up to the demands of life. You think it's your own fault because you don't try hard enough. This leads to the task of not allowing oneself to be abused as a scapegoat.

Helpful stones for coping with this task are, for example: Chrysoprase, Rainbow Obsidian, Epidote

Chrysoprase strengthens the nerves and helps with feelings of inferiority, because it makes us confident and gives us joy (joy drives the wheels! Goethe). Thus it helps in the job search by arming us against discouragement and helping us not to give up.

Rainbow Obsidian works against negative energy from other people, e.g. envious people, schemers, cheats, thieves, competitors, bullying colleagues and so on.

Epidote strengthens the nerves and helps against stress.

The **northeast** symbolises education / self-education. Should there be a toilet, kitchen, storage room, a missing or additional area in the NE of our home, we might have a problem, depending on and in combination with our personal Feng Shui, because the NE does not fit harmoniously into the floor plan of our home and / or is only available to us in a limited way. Then we probably lack the attention and care of the environment and as a result we lack the awareness of ourselves. We have to play a role and are not perceived as a human being at all. We are expected to want what we are supposed to want. This results in the task of being able to accept oneself as one is, to find one's own centre.

Helpful stones for mastering this task are, for example: Tourmaline, Amethyst, Calzite

All **tourmalines** ground or centre. They act like a fountain of youth and give optimism. Black tourmaline is also said to protect against electrosmog.

Amethyst helps with self-discovery, expansion of consciousness and personality development.

Calzites bring the aura into balance.

For energy vampirism, **rainbow obsidian** helps together with the visualisation of being enveloped in a white cloak of light with a zip. Zip the cloak from the bottom to the top whenever you meet the person who is sucking you dry.

The **east** symbolises health / family. Should there be a toilet, kitchen, storage room, a missing or additional area in the east of our home, we could have a problem, depending on and in combination with our personal Feng Shui, because the east does not fit harmoniously into the layout of our home and / or is only available to us in a limited way. Then we probably lack independence, clarity, carefreeness, health and well-being. Thoughts may always revolve around one and the same family drama. Despair spreads. There is no way out. This leads to the task of conquering 'memory demons' (post-traumatic stress disorder) and freeing oneself from addictions and illusions.

Helpful stones for overcoming this task are, for example: Tiger eye, labradorite, fluorite, onyx, jasper, blood stone.

Tiger's eye protects against overexertion and brings clarity to messy situations.
Labradorite integrates traumas and heals old wounds.
Fluorite improves access to the subconscious.
Onyx improves self-perception and dream perception.
Jasper strengthens courage and assertiveness.
Blood stone strengthens the immune system, grounds and helps to 'let go of control'. One gains new confidence and can sleep better as a result.

The **southeast** symbolises wealth. Should there be a toilet, kitchen, storeroom, misplaced or additional area in the SE of our home, we might have a problem in terms of wealth, depending and in combination with our personal Feng Shui. Wealth includes the whole quality of life: prosperity, comfort, satisfying relationships. If the SE does not fit harmoniously into the layout of our home and / or is only available to us in a limited way, then we may lack satisfying communication. We present ourselves to the outside world differently than we actually are, think and feel. This results in disturbed communication. Our counterpart feels the inconsistency and struggles with the contradiction, thus wasting energy. There is no mutual exchange of energy. Wealth is based on the free flow of energies of all participants (so-called win/win situation). Accordingly, this results in the task for us to take off our 'mask' and become authentic. Helpful stones for mastering this task are, for example: Gold topaz, pyrite, jadeite, gagat/jet, sodalite.

Gold topaz gives self-confidence, through it we dare to take off our mask. Through self-confidence and inner strength one attracts wealth, well-being and love.
Pyrite is considered a wish stone. It connects us with the spiritual level, i.e. with what we really wish for and in this way helps to create material abundance.
Jadeite attracts luck in financial matters.
Gagat/Jet helps to jump over one's own shadow, to overcome loss, causes discipline and responsibility and thus helps to reduce debts.

Sodalite is the communication stone and helps to find the right words.

The **south** symbolises fame and recognition. Should there be a toilet, kitchen, storage room, a missing or additional area in the S of our home, we could have a problem, depending on and in combination with our personal Feng Shui, because the S does not fit harmoniously into the floor plan of our home and / or is only available to us in a limited way. Then we probably lack appreciation and recognition of our person and performance. It follows that we have to stop 'hiding our light under a bushel' in order to be noticed. How do we do that? If we stop trying to get recognition mainly by conforming, then we will also reject external regulations that constrain and frustrate us. This gives us the task of first reflecting on ourselves and finding out what we are enthusiastic about, so that we can then stand up for ourselves, claim our place and demand what is rightfully ours.

Helpful stones for mastering this task are, for example: Ruby, citrine, carnelian.

Ruby promotes self-love and creativity.

Citrine acts as a sunstone, thereby strengthening our charisma.

Carnelian gives new energy and vitality.

The **southwest** symbolises love and relationships. If there is a toilet, kitchen, storage room, a missing or additional area in the SW of our home, we could have a problem, depending on and in combination with our personal Feng Shui, because the SW does not fit harmoniously into the floor plan of our home and / or is only available to us in a limited way. Then we probably lack peace of mind because we live in a difficult relationship or are unintentionally single. It follows that we have the task of bringing order into the chaos of our emotions. How do we do this? We should start by writing down our dreams in order to find our dream partner in the dream. One recognises the dream partner by the fact that he/she brings us back our peace of mind.

Helpful stones for accomplishing this task are, for example: Moonstone, rose quartz, jade.

Moonstone provides access to the emotional world.
Rose quartz exudes peace, helps to achieve serenity and calm.
Jade is a lucky charm in every respect and a healing stone.

The **west** symbolises children. Should there be a toilet, kitchen, storage room, a missing or additional area in the W of our home, we could have a problem, depending on and in combination with our personal Feng Shui, because the W does not fit harmoniously into the floor plan of our home and / or is only available to us in a limited way. Then we probably lack lightness, play and fun in life. Burdens press down on our shoulders. Everything is so serious and heavy. We are expected to carry the whole burden alone. As a result, we have to learn to recognise unjustified impositions, to set limits, to let go and to relax. How do we do that? Our body helps us. Let's use it as a mirror of our circumstances. It gives us unlimited power if we know how to make it serve us. Meditation helps us to read the body like a book, so that we can recognise the intentions behind events and adjust to them.

Helpful stones for accomplishing this task include: Turquoise, aventurine, blue chalcedony.

Turquoise protects the soul by guarding against injustices such as impositions, unjustified attacks and criticism.

Aventurine is the balance stone par excellence (Yin / Yang). It helps us to consider the balance of give and take.

Blue chalcedony is considered a lucky charm, it stabilises the aura, gives one the 'thick skin'.

If you want to actively cope with one or the other of the tasks mentioned here and get the corresponding stones, use them e.g. as a pendant, as a trouser pocket stone, put them under the pillow. They should be cleaned regularly under running lukewarm water (except selenite and haematite) and recharged in a clear crystal quartz group before the next use. Be intuitive in your choice of stones. You may find other stones that help you. The stone that catches our eye or magically attracts us is always the right one.
The stones are most effective when you feel them on your skin. Take a stone in your hand that speaks to you, withdraw and meditate with it. Depending on which stone you use, you will feel its vibrations as tingling, prickling, numbness, warmth or like a current flowing through you. In this case, concentrate on the feeling and you will notice how it spreads through your body and into your aura and makes you feel good. The stone fills up your 'empty batteries' with its vibrations and thus has a therapeutic effect. In many cases we can treat ourselves. Mother Earth helps us with this.

Meditation: Journey to the Underworld

Self-awareness is the only thing that can save us. When we become aware of our own spiritual needs, we change our destiny.
A journey into the underworld under the protection of the magical stone circle is one of the things that can help us with self-knowledge.
The best time for this meditation is at dusk, when the worlds are separating, and of course at full moon, after we have drawn the moon down on us.

Let's make sure we are undisturbed for a while before we begin. We need a compass with which we can determine the points of the compass. We draw the magic circle by placing a pebble of about the same size in each cardinal direction. We lay out the circle large enough on the ground so that we can meditate in it. We take a selenite rod or obelisk in our hands. It acts as an antenna and amplifier of the magical force field of the stones. We sit down in the centre of the circle in our meditation posture. We clasp the selenite with both hands and breathe deeply, slowly drawing deeper and deeper into ourselves with each breath until we are calm and relaxed. We close our eyes and turn our perception inwards. With the question of what is missing for our happiness and our salvation, we feel ourselves in.

Now imagine you are going down a flight of stairs. At the bottom you stand in front of a door. Behind the door is your lucky place. Open the door. Go through the door.
Now visualise in your mind's eye your 'auspicious place' or 'inner garden', according to your imagination, look around and explore the place more closely. Somewhere you discover a clearing or a round place or a stone circle in the middle of which a tree stands or a fire burns or a fountain bubbles. To the left of it is a stage or platform with a black curtain and a silver moon. Walk towards the curtain. The curtain opens, you step through into an unlimited space and behind you the curtain closes. You look around you. You can feel the presence of the Goddess,

but you cannot see her. She is shapeless. You kneel down and bow in deep humility.

You now ask the Goddess for what you are lacking for your salvation. The Goddess blesses you and you thank her for her blessing by placing your palms together and touching your third eye with your fingertips with your palms closed. You rise and slowly turn around and open your hands. At the same time the curtain opens in front of you and you go back through it to the place from which you came. Once there, you look at everything carefully for a while until you see something that is meant for you. It may be an object, a symbol or perhaps a person, an animal or a plant. Whatever it is, it is there for your peace of mind. You accept it gratefully. You attach a symbol somewhere on your body, you take an object, a plant or a stone to yourself, you take a person trustingly by the hand, you ask an animal to accompany you.

Now slowly leave the place the same way you came. Go through the door, close it behind you and go up the stairs again. At the top you gradually come back to the present. Breathe deeply several times and open your eyes. Be aware of your surroundings until you are fully awake again. Then open the magic circle by bowing to the guardians of the cardinal points, symbolised by the stones, before collecting the stones. Think no more about it and resume your daily routine.

The whole process should not take longer than 15 minutes.

It won't take long before you suddenly remember what you are still missing for your happiness, so that you can now consciously strive for it. No matter what situation you find yourself in, create the vision of this happiness and paint it in bright colours in your imagination. Then reprogramme yourself by means of autosuggestion.

Autosuggestion:

Create for yourself the intention that matches your vision like this:

'I choose to remain unimpressed by my nightmares'; 'I choose to get enough money to support myself'; 'I choose to remain unimpressed by N. N.'s (person's name) emotional abuse'; 'I choose to be grateful for my life'; 'I choose to find a satisfying relationship'; and so on - depending on what is still missing for your happiness, think it out for yourself.

It is important to start the sentence with 'I choose' and to phrase it positively.

By allowing yourself to choose, you empower yourself to consciously shape your own destiny.

From now on, always use your self-created intention when challenged by the shadow and repeat it as often as necessary to defeat the shadow.

In everyday life, too, always consciously choose your decisions in the spirit of your self-created vision. Pay attention to 'impeccability' (Castaneda). This means: *Beware of feeling like an immortal being who has all the time on earth and acts accordingly, because the feeling of having time is foolish. There are no survivors on this earth. A warrior has time only for his immaculateness. Everything else saps his strength. Immaculate action recharges it.* (Castaneda) Anyone who has mastered this 'inner martial art' is a 'warrior'.

Magic

Magic is an independent energy given to us to avert 'evil' events. (Hornung) Magic *(heka)* works with the force that balances between opposites, with the Ma'at. Through magic, the knowing magician brings about peace of mind.

Fear is a strong force. It spurs us on to learn. Panic, on the other hand, paralyses, because panic means: the soul moves away. A shaman / magician / witch trains his intention (will / spirit) by learning to control his thoughts, to transform tormenting emotions and to make the right decision. Accordingly, the skill to be acquired in spiritual terms is: 'to make a weapon out of illness' or to practise 'inner martial arts' when dealing with one's character or, as Castaneda puts it, to lose the *'human form'*, i.e. to transform emotions and to conquer desire until it becomes subservient to one. The lesson is called: When desires are not in harmony with Ma'at, selflessness frees you from the pain caused by the ego. Then accept what is without rebelling against it. Desires that are not in harmony with Ma'at cause suffering. Suffering in life is purification - purgatory. The only remedy is desirelessness, because *'desirelessness liberates from suffering'* (Buddha). In this case, one ends suffering by bringing one's existence back in line with the divine order (Ma'at) through impeccability, i.e. by avoiding letting oneself go. Note: Getting something fulfilled or not getting it fulfilled can be equally disappointing both times.

Magic is soul strength or personal power in the face of opponents in the struggle for existence, but light beings also replace lacking soul strength in harmony with the power that balances (Ma'at). (For more details on this, see my book: Die Lichtwesen des Tarot).
One works magically through 'knowing' - recognising the right thing in harmony with Ma'at; 'wanting' - testing the will; 'choosing' - making a decision; 'daring' - e.g. daring the ritual, the action and 'silence'.

Magic is also feasible in the following order:
1. Transformation of suffering into relaxation, e.g. through selflessness.
2. During the day, one goes into the alpha state in meditation (e.g. according to Silva) and makes contact with the Higher Self in the Otherworld.
3. At night, the soul in the Otherworld / Underworld takes over the execution in the lucid dream.
4. Reality changes in its own sense.

Note: Magicians / shamans / witches solve their drive conflicts in fantasy by watching their dream body (soul) create the healing reality in the underworld / astral world. But which reality is the salvific one is determined by the Ma'at.

Oracle

We recognise the direction of the power that works in our relationships in secret by consulting the oracle in a certain way. For this purpose we lay out the 'Square of Jupiter' with the court cards of the Tarot. We lay out the present family and the family of origin separately.

The questioner takes the court cards in the left hand, shuffles and lays them out side by side from right to left as a field, 4 cards in a row under the other. The people lying horizontally next to each other in a row are in balance with each other (give and take is balanced). The people lying vertically in a row below each other are in imbalance with the healing direction of the force working from the top downwards. If you are on top, it means that you owe appreciation, respect, honour, cooperation, and so on. to the people below you, because otherwise you will have the Ma'at against you.

Example interpretation Present family:

Jack of Swords	Jack of Coins	Queen of Cups	Jack of Staff
Knight of Swords	Knight of Wands	Queen of the Staff	King of Swords
Queen of Swords	King of the coins	Queen of the coins	Knight of Coins
Jack of Cups	King of Cups	Knight of Cups	King of Wands

The family includes the living and the dead. As can be seen here, the Queen of Cups in this case owes appreciation, respect, deference, assistance, and so on to those vertically below her, i.e. she is obliged to serve, if she does not want to go against the direction of the force determined by the Ma'at and whom she would then have against her, which would lead to great problems, sufferings, and so on.

If you have people lying vertically under you who have already died, you must take them into your heart to give them the honour they deserve, only then will you receive their blessing and the direction of the force can change.
A detailed explanation of the effect of the direction of the force can be found in my book: Die Richtung der Kraft – Familienrepräsentation mit Tarot.

Assignment of the court cards to persons in the family of origin and the present family:

Family of origin
Queen of staff - maternal grandmother of the questioner
Staff King - grandmother's brother or father
Staff Knight - grandmother's male relative
Staff Jack/Page - grandmother's female relative

Coin King - maternal grandfather
Coin Queen - grandfather's mother or sister
Coin Knight - grandfather's male relative
Coin Page/Jack - grandfather female relative

Sword King - Father
Sword-Queen - mother or sister of the father
Knight of Swords - paternal male relative
Jack of Swords/Page - paternal female relative

Cup Queen - Mother
Cup King - brother or half-brother of the mother
Cup Knight - maternal male relative
Cup Jack/Page - maternal female relative

Present family
Queen of staff - mother of the partner
Staff King - brother or father of the partner's mother

Staff Knight - maternal male relative of the partner or former partner of the female
Staff Jack/Page - maternal female relative of the partner

Coin King - father of the partner
Coin Queen - mother or sister of the partner's father
Coin Knight - paternal male relative of the partner
Coin Jack/Page - paternal female relatives of the partner or former partners of the man

Sword King - Man
Sword Queen - sister of the man or former wife
Knight of Swords - male children or nephews of the man
Jack of Swords/Page - female children or nieces of the man

Cup Queen - Woman
Cup King - brother of the woman or former husband
Cup Knight - male children or nephews of the woman
Cup Jack/Page - female children or nieces of the woman

First aid for 'demon' attack

'Demon' of paralysis

Associated shadows can be: Fatigue, exhaustion and numbness, hatred, anger as well as primal fears of losing love, being outcast; fears of death such as: being helplessly at the mercy of others, being frozen in terror, fear of being at the mercy of others; through supposed feelings of guilt, not being able to defend oneself; emotions of being locked up, like being paralysed, despondency.

Liberation and balancing takes place through acceptance, surrender, abandonment, forgiveness and comes from the realisation: "I am!" - which is the regaining of primal trust, because with this realisation one overcomes the separation from oneself. In the case of negative emotions, a combination of breathing exercises and meditations is useful to achieve relaxation, that is, the subsiding of the pain.

Breathing exercise:
In case of tension, one should exhale into this pain and thereby perceive the emotion, i.e. open oneself to the pain, get into it (abandon oneself to it, disappear into it, only be pain = let go of fear).
This usually results in relaxation. Relaxation is the union between emotion and consciousness and thus the realisation of the intention that was originally hidden behind the tension. But if the emotion can be called by its name, the separation from oneself is already overcome.

Meditation - Intention of forgiveness:
This involves inwardly repeating the appropriate forgiveness intention for about 15 minutes or as long as necessary, also in combination with each other:
"I forgive myself." "I forgive my life situation." "I forgive my work situation." "I forgive my relationship situation." "I forgive my financial situation." "I forgive my parents." - and so on. (Everyone thinks of the forgiveness intention that suits their situation).

Ground:
Sit on a chair or the edge of a chair (small people). Keep the back straight, feet firmly on the floor, legs forming a right angle at the knee. Inhale deeply and hold the breath for a moment. Exhaling press the feet firmly against the floor. Tense the thigh muscles and the pelvic floor. Release the tension. Repeat the process several times for as long as it is comfortable. In this way we revitalise our root chakra.

Helpful stones: Agate, haematite, jasper, garnet, ruby, all red stones.
Aromatherapy: citronella, eucalyptus, pine, rosemary, lemon.

'Demon' of compulsion

Associated shadows (negative emotions) can be: jealousy, sadness, frustration, stress, inability to feel anything, or uncontrolled emotionality such as 'bursting into tears'; hysteria, worry, longing, exaggerated sexual fantasies, sex addiction, the tendency to prioritise one's own sexual gratification, repressed urges or constant longing for fulfilling sexuality.

Liberation and balance in personal imbalances is achieved by turning to one's own 'spiritual ideal' (Cayce), to one's own centre; being in one's own element.
If we assume that the body is the temple of our spirit, our ideal is always potentially contained in our body when we are united with ourselves, in harmony or in balance with ourselves. Ask yourself what is really important to you in life. What would you strive for if you could? Ultimately, what we get when we find our 'spiritual ideal' is nothing other than well-being, health and identity.

Centre meditation:
Lie on your back, then place a snow obsidian a hand's width below the navel on the pubic bone (sacral chakra) on bare skin, the clear crystal quartz on the forehead (brow chakra). Use stones at least the size of a walnut. Inhale and exhale, and concentrate on the rhythm of the breath, relax and imagine *"how the obsidian radiates from the pubic bone backwards to the coccyx and the rock crystal from the forehead into the entire skull."* (Hodosi) The spine connects the two chakras as a ray of light. Feel the two points of the body where the

stones rest and abandon yourself to this feeling at these two poles, don't think of anything but just feel into it. The goal of the meditation is reached as soon as you feel your inner body brighten up (or become pleasantly warm). You are in your centre again.

Helpful stones: Carnelian, moonstone, snow obsidian, clear crystal quartz, all orange stones.
Aromatherapy: rosewood, tarragon, rose, aniseed.

'Demon' of fear

The demon of fear tempts us to suppress vital desires and feelings. This increasingly results in the emotion of being overwhelmed and irritable, which in turn flows outwards and permanently disrupts relationships with the opposite sex and in professional life, resulting in unhappiness.
Negative emotions can be: Nausea, helpless nervousness, inner restlessness, paranoia, envy, feelings of powerlessness, 'nervous irritability', overactivity.

Liberation and balance come through education through enlightenment in relation to oneself and the world, and self-awareness. In this case, one must manage the feat of 'pulling oneself out of the swamp by one's own hair' - creating an inner space. This can only be achieved by 'broadening one's spiritual horizon' or by strengthening the power of one's own mind.

Breathing exercise:
This Sufi breathing exercise has a calming effect: simply count to 7 internally while inhaling, hold the breath on 8, then count from the beginning while exhaling until the number 7 is reached, hold the breath on 8, inhale again while counting to 7, and so on. This breathing exercise can be done in any position and for as long as you like.

It is particularly helpful to consciously direct the breath to areas of the body that are painful or tense. Concentrate on the tense area and breathe in and out through the nose. In the imagination, direct the exhalation directly into the tense area and exhale twice as long as you inhale. Repeat the process as long as necessary. Usually this is meditation enough to achieve a result: The pain dissolves.

Light meditation:
We hold the left nostril closed with the index finger of the right hand and breathe in white light through the right nostril, counting to 7. Then we hold our breath and let the light circle in our imagination in the stomach area while we count to 7 again.
Now we open the left nostril and close the right nostril with the right thumb, while we exhale through the left nostril and count to 7. Imagine dark clouds escaping through the left nostril.
Now we inhale white light through the left nostril while counting to 7. We hold the breath, count to 7 and let the white light circle in the stomach area.
Now we open the right nostril and close the left nostril with the index finger of the right hand .... as above.
Practise alternate nasal breathing with the idea of white light until you feel calm and relaxed again, or until the shadows you exhale become lighter and lighter.

Healing meditation while lying down: *'I consciously activate my solar plexus chakra'.* Imagine inhaling golden light into the stomach area. While exhaling, let the golden light circle in the upper abdomen. Repeat the intention inwardly. Inhale golden light again and so on until the body sensation changes and the upper abdomen area gives a feeling of warmth. Now let the golden light spread throughout the body and give up conscious breathing. Enjoy the stream of light for a little while. Then close the solar chakra by imagining an open golden lotus flower closing its leaves.

Helpful stones: Tiger eye, amber, precious topaz, citrine, kunzite and all yellow stones.
Aromatherapy: lavender, galbanum, basil, bergamot, coriander, mint, rosemary.

'Demon' of the imagination

Demon influences can manifest in: Worry, not being able to say 'no', self-exploitation as well as 'being exploited'. Shadows can be: Arrogance, mockery, coldness, apathy, heartlessness, inability to open up for fear of rejection, as well as hatred, egoism, imperiousness, palpitations or the impression 'the heart stops'.

Liberation and balance comes through applying the 'right measure' in dealing with the environment.
,Give' and 'take' come from the heart - accept yourself, love yourself as you are and you will be able to receive and let go in equal measure.

Transformational Light Meditation:
When you are undisturbed, get into a comfortable position and breathe deeply for several breaths. Then imagine a green glow in your chest that gradually spreads throughout your body. Now, in addition, imagine a green glow spreading in your head and connecting with the green glow in your chest. Feel yourself enveloped and immersed in deep green for a few moments. Now ask your synchronised green self to transform the negative emotions in your body. Name the negative emotion or the part of your body that is tense or painful. For example: *"I ask my synchronised green self to transform the pain in the left side of my body."* Repeat this sentence until you clearly experience a physical feedback. This can be a colour change. It may be a word that suddenly comes into your awareness. It can simply be the easing of tension, of pain. Whatever it is, it has to change the body feeling. With the change of the body feeling towards the

positive, the purpose of meditation is fulfilled. If there is no change in the emotion, repeat the process with a blue glow (violet glow, white glow).

Self-love light meditation while lying down: like the breathing exercise on p. 55 but with the idea of white light, which we inhale and direct into the corresponding part of the body with each exhalation. In doing so, we see our inner being as a cave flooded with light and we ourselves transform into a healing energy stream of white light. We give attention and healing energy to each part of the body with the exhalation and see the respective part of the body radiating gratefully back to us. Afterwards, we give up conscious breathing and rest for a while before resuming everyday life.

Helpful stones: Rose quartz, aventurine, kunzite, emerald, jade, all pink and green stones.
Aromatherapy: rose oil, camomile, lavender, neroli, orange, sandalwood.

'Demon' of despair

Prevalent shadows can be: "lump in the throat", "the throat feels tight", stuttering or half-baked ranting, being intimidated, cowering, hopelessness, 'inner emptiness', loneliness, feelings of guilt, compulsive mulling, acting under the control of others.

Compensation takes place, for example, with meditation, yoga, conscious breath control, autogenic training, and so on. One must develop body and emotional awareness. This means that you have to constantly reflect on your emotions; localise emotions in the body; consciously breathe into emotions, perceive them, accept them and call them by name. Liberation takes place through breath control and "putting oneself into" the secrets of the body (subconscious), which are also the secrets of the world, e.g. by means of dream interpretation, recognising external determination, seeking out the dream partner.

Breath control:
It is particularly helpful to consciously direct the breath to areas of the body that are painful or tense. Concentrate on the tense area and breathe in and out through the nose. In your imagination, direct your exhalation directly into the tense area and exhale twice as long as you inhale. Repeat the process as long as necessary.

Healing meditation while lying down: *'I consciously activate my throat chakra'*. Imagine inhaling blue light. While exhaling, let the blue light circle in the throat and shoulder area.

Repeat the intention inwardly. Inhale blue light again and so on until the body sensation changes and the neck and shoulder area with the throat chakra gives a feeling of freedom and expansiveness. Now let the blue light spread throughout the body and give up conscious breathing. Enjoy the stream of light for a little while. Then close the throat chakra by imagining how an open blue lotus flower closes its leaves.

Zen meditation:
Go for a walk in nature. Just walk and just breathe. As soon as thoughts, memories and so on claim your attention, give them a name and enclose them in a transparent bubble. Let this bubble float away and, if you like, let it burst like a soap bubble.
Return your attention to your breathing and walking and stay in the 'here and now'.

In this way, one can gradually make all unpleasant thoughts, especially obsessive thoughts, emotions and people who suggestively harass one, disappear from one's consciousness. To make them gradually disappear from your life as well, imagine your 'inner retreat' or 'inner garden', remember the unpleasant things, wish them well, enclose them in a bubble, let them float away and burst. Repeat this performance as often as you like, especially when the unpleasant things want to come back. At some point they no longer bother you.

Transformational light meditation: see above

Helpful stones: Aquamarine, turquoise, chalcedony, all blue stones.

Aromatherapy: Anise, marjoram, mint, orange, rosemary.

Autosuggestion: *I choose to remain unimpressed by my despair.*

'Letting go' mantra: *I am grateful that everything has dissolved into goodness.*

,Demon' of depression

This demon causes feelings of powerlessness, depression, headache, listlessness, inability to think clearly, delusions.

Liberation and balancing takes place through conscious thought guidance.
By means of his thoughts and their effect on will and imagination, man creates his own reality, therefore it becomes necessary here, if one wants to improve anything in his life, to first regularly act on negative emotions by means of transformation light meditation. One uses the frequencies of the long-wave brain waves such as green, blue, purple, white.
Furthermore, one should avoid the daily 'brainwashing' in front of the TV set, especially of commercials and entertainment programmes as often as possible, in order to avoid the 'anaesthesia' and thus distraction from oneself.
In addition, one should practise conscious mind control, e.g. by means of Zen meditation, see above.
Ritual - Invocation of a Spirit (p. 56)
Healing meditation while lying down: *'I consciously activate my brow chakra'*. Imagine breathing in midnight blue colour. While exhaling, let the dark blue colour circle in the forehead and head area. Repeat the intention continuously. Inhale the dark blue colour again and so on until the body sensation changes and the pressure disappears from the forehead and head area. Now let the dark blue colour spread throughout the body and stop breathing consciously.

Stay immersed in deep dark blue for a little while. Then close the brow chakra by imagining an open dark blue lotus flower closing its leaves.
Helpful stones: lapis lazuli, sapphire, sodalite, all dark blue stones.
Aromatherapy: Cedar, parsley, neroli, lemongrass.

Tarot Card Reading (Major Arcanum)
for the purpose of recognising the situation in the hidden reality

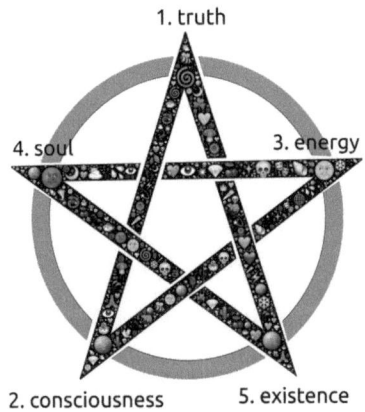

1. truth
4. soul
3. energy
2. consciousness
5. existence

or: 1. health, 2. happiness, 3. love, 4. karma, 5. wealth
or: 1. appointment, 2. exercise, 3. nutrition, 4. self-love, 5. place of strength

Demon' of insecurity

This demon causes restlessness, inner restlessness, fear of death, emotions of meaninglessness and inferiority.

Liberation and relief comes through dance, music, yoga and meditation.

Belly dance meditation:
Belly dance meditation consists of consciously directing our attention to the movement while dancing. We do the movement and at the same time concentrate on that part of our body where the movement is happening. It is about a gentle, effortless resting of perception and attention. If we keep this up consistently, we are completely with ourselves. Once again, the essential thing is to focus conscious attention on the perception of the movement. This helps us to feel, appreciate and empathise with our body in the 'here and now'.
Feel into yourself and the movement, consciously perceive your body with the question in your heart: what happens to me when I make this movement?
No matter which perceptions become conscious, they are all shifted towards pleasure if we accept them. For example, if we encounter pain, we should not fight it or reject it, but accept the pain and try out different changes and movement corrections that alleviate the pain sensation in the direction of pleasure.
In the long run, this way of dancing can enhance the performance of all our senses and give us an intense sense of well-being.

Breathing exercise:
Directing the breath means directing attention. For relaxation, every day when you have time for yourself, or in the evening before going to sleep, direct your attention to your body while lying or standing, by breathing deeply in and out as follows:

Inhale into the heart, exhale into the soles of the feet, three times.
Inhale into the heart, exhale into the knees, three times.
Inhale into the heart, exhale into the pelvic floor, three times.
Inhale into the heart, exhale into the hips, three times.
Inhale into the heart, exhale into the navel, three times.
Inhale into the heart, exhale into the diaphragm, three times.
Inhale into the heart, exhale into the shoulders, three times.
Inhale into the heart, exhale into the throat, three times.
Inhale into the heart, exhale into the crown of the head, three times.
Inhale into the heart, exhale into the palms, three times.
Inhale into the heart, exhale into the heart, three times.

In this way, you train your awareness of yourself and find it easier in everyday life to be mindful, to perceive your belly feeling and to follow your instinct.

Helpful stones: Amethyst, clear crystal quartz, all white and violet stones.
Aromatherapy: Ylang-ylang, bergamot, jasmine, coriander, clove, lemon.
Ritual: Break a curse (see p. 57)
Autosuggestion: *I choose to remember myself.*

Rituals

Invocation of a spirit

Observe your negative thoughts for one day and write them down on a piece of paper. At dusk, draw the magic circle of protection around you by drawing a standing pentagram clockwise in the air in all four directions with your index finger or wand. Start in the east, then follow south, west, north. Protected in this way, burn the note in a fireproof container (e.g. large ashtray) and in this way hand over all your negative thoughts to the spirit of fire. Speak while the note is burning:

Spirit of fire take the thoughts

that bind me,

transform them and break the chains,

give me clarity and help save me.

Repeat the chant as long as the fire burns. When the paper has burnt down, thank the spirit of the fire, say goodbye to it, open the magic circle by drawing a standing pentagram counterclockwise in the air around you with your index finger or wand in all four cardinal directions. Start in the east, then north, west, south. This opens the circle and releases the summoned spirit of fire.

Break a curse I

Salt helps with curses. Mix a big bottle of salt water and the next time you shower, pour it over your head. Make sure that the water washes off your whole body. Imagine how everything that is negatively attached to you disappears down the drain with the salt water. To do this, say a rhyming cleansing phrase. It is best if you think up the saying yourself. But you can also use my saying (see below). Then thank the great goddess or Mother Earth for her help and make a donation to the nearest animal shelter. This should take care of the matter.

Spirit of the earth, take away the curse,
that found me.
Transform him, let me recover.
Take him back! -
Fortunately for me, I am now free.
And that's fine, that's how it should be.

Break a curse II

Draw the magic circle of protection around you at dusk. Get into your meditation posture and breathe deeply several times until you are calm and relaxed. Close your eyes and visualise the curse in the form of an upside down black pentagram. Now direct a beam of pure glistening white light from you towards the pentagram. See how the pentagram gradually turns from the head to the feet and becomes brilliant white. The curse is broken. End the meditation.

Neutrino power in ancient Egypt

Pyramids in the dimensions of the Cheops pyramid are zero-point energy converters (Chi converters). When an object is placed in the centre of the pyramid, the molecules of the object are aligned in the sense of the original order. The object then attracts the chi (neutrinos) like an antenna. The example of the broken razor blade, whose structure realigned itself at the point of breakage in the pyramid experiment, is generally regarded as proof. Neutrinos (Chi) are everywhere in the universe. They are where physics speaks of vacuum (space) and they are faster than light.

Black holes swallow everything including light and the only thing that comes out are neutrinos. If pyramids are neutrino power converters and they are all over the earth, then once upon a time in a lost global civilisation, as in ancient Egypt, the intention was to make chi available for the purpose of healing.
Chi is life force. Sex is life force. Chi / life force is the only energy we possess. This is why the shaman Castaneda recommends that we be stingy with sex.

Sex and the meaning of life

Castaneda speaks of three realms: the known (this world/boredom), the unknown (underworld/ adventure), the unknowable (unlimited/lack of orientation / chaos).

The will / spirit belongs to the unknown.

The unknowable or unlimited is governed by the Ma'at according to the ideas of the ancient Egyptians.

Castaneda says: *We only see what we would have learned to see. We see a world of objects. In reality, out there are the emanations of the eagle.*

The eagle is Castaneda's symbol for the unknowable, the unlimited of the ancient Egyptians, which is governed by the Ma'at.

The purpose of life is the expansion of consciousness (self-creation), to spiritualise oneself. Castaneda distinguishes three states of consciousness:
- Awareness matured through experience =
  1. attention
- Body consciousness = 2. attention
- Enlightenment (inner fire) = 3. attention

The eagle gives consciousness and eats it up again. The eagle can be felt with the body.
The purpose of sex is to generate life. Through sex, the eagle gives consciousness to the child.
By having children, one diminishes the ardour of consciousness in oneself. (Castaneda)

Furthermore, Castaneda speaks of the 'ally'. The ally is that which is connected to one's own existence.

In Busson, the 'guardian' and the 'shadow' are the two sides of the 'ally', the immortal part of the self / spirit, the Higher Self.

The guardian / the 'guardian of the threshold' / the guardian spirit is the immortal part of the self.

The 'immortal part of the self' is the spirit form from previous incarnations, a form that warns you, protects you, helps you at the crossroads (in Busson the figure of 'Ewli').

The shadow / the dark is the part of the immortal self from mistakes / sins and the acquired unredeemed traumas of this and all previous lives (in Busson the figure of the 'Fangerl').

Paul Busson: *'Dying without losing consciousness succeeds when, while dying, you concentrate on the firm will to remember everything'*.

The security of the soul

Sexuality (body) is man's transmission belt for the knowledge of himself, his soul, love, life. Sexual urges must be learned to analyse. They serve man as fuel for the spirit.

Even the Bible still contains, albeit completely disguised, a reference to the acquisition of knowledge about oneself. We all know the allegory of the snake and the apple from the tree of knowledge.

But contrary to the Bible's assertion that the serpent is the 'devil', 'eating the apple from the tree of knowledge' actually means learning to question sexuality and recognising the soul (serpent / chi = life force). The snake is the soul! But the soul follows the Ma'at, the great Goddess! As long as man does not know his soul, he is in danger of falling into the trap and suffering.

The allegory in the Bible says exactly: By listening to your soul (*snake*), which communicates with you through your body (e.g. gut feeling, sexuality, frustration, emotion, illness, and so on - *Tree of Knowledge!*), you become aware of your needs (*apple*). You perceive your needs yourself by recognising (*eating*) them = consciousness. Now you are able to make the right decisions and take responsibility for yourself.

Or, to put it another way with Edgar Cayce: *'Spirit is more than consciousness. Consciousness arises only in incarnation through the application of will to desire'.*

The body is the transmission belt for the spirit. Whenever sex happens without love, the life force (soul) is weakened and thus the spirit / will is darkened. Then one has no more assertiveness in the unknown / in the underworld (in the subtle / in the astral world). One no longer has magic. One can no longer do magic. No one acts for you in the underworld. Instead of the spirit, fear (shadow / negativity) moves into the body. The **mounting point** (Castaneda) shifts.

The mounting point is the inner support, the reference point, the centre, is what holds us together at the core, constitutes our world view, is the basis for the compensated balance. Shifting the mounting point does not mean simply changing the perspective, but realigning the will, adapting to changed circumstances, changing the inner attitude, revising a wrong decision.

In the case of an unintentional shift due to external circumstances, because the balance changes, such as existential contradiction, bullying, loss of a loved one, adultery, and so on, there is a threat of disorientation, confusion, danger. The gap in the energy body arises through which death can occur.

To enter into death means: to enter into time. To enter into time means: to enter into change. Time changes everything, including words. The only thing that stops death is consciousness.

Impeccability consists in recognising the limits or fault lines of one's own character and overcoming them with the help of the opposing force (the Ma'at), then we also control destiny. It is precisely for this purpose, namely to learn to recognise fate or our character and thus to influence it, that we have been thrown into physical existence by fate itself. This existence is only the further development of the previous one.

Therefore, with sexual desires, always ask yourself: *"Do they bring warmth, light? Or do they bring sickness, hatred and fear?"* (Cayce) For only if they bring the warmth, the light, are they in harmony with your spirit and serve your life.

Belly dancing and meditation are good for the spirit because the shadows can be brought into consciousness and thus the will can be realigned or adapted to changed circumstances.

Before one dies, one should still see one's soul in the underworld during one's lifetime or free the spirit from shadows / negativity and in this way create the dream body, only then one is also safe in the hereafter, i.e. protected from the second death, the *'disintegration of the ethereal body into fragments that drift apart'* (Sagan).

Witch dance is ecstatic dance

Many amateur belly dancers appreciate the value that belly dance has not only for physical health but also for mental health. This value lies in its psychological-spiritual dimension, which reveals itself to the belly dancer when she practices the dance as meditation and allows herself to be completely captured by the melody, rhythm and her own movement.

Since belly dancing originates from ecstasy cults of nomadic tribes in Africa and the Orient and is therefore an ancient method to unite body and mind and to come back to oneself, you can perfectly switch off in stressful situations if you put your favourite music in the CD player and simply belly dance to the rhythms. "But I can do that with any music and any dance," you might say now. But belly dance has an effect precisely on the *"three narrows"* (Wilhelm Reich) of the body and specifically dissolves blockages of energy (= emotions repressed into the unconscious) there. This cannot be said of any dance style.
The type of movement consists of isolated shaking, pushing, circling, tilting, lifting, lowering, trembling (shimmy) of body parts, while the rest of the body remains in a resting position. In this way, each part of the body interacts individually with gravity. This is a real challenge and must be practised regularly.

The *"three constrictions"* Reich describes are in the pelvic floor, the diaphragm and the neck area. They are places where ring muscles do their work. These are muscles that surround an opening in a ring because something has to be closed temporarily (for example, anus, mouth, eyelid, urinary bladder, iris). The first thing that becomes noticeable at the "three narrows" is cramps when we repress emotions. In the course of time, even body deformations develop there. What does that mean exactly? It means that the body always acts and flows with gravity. If the energy cannot flow in certain parts of the body because blockages have occurred there, the person forms a compensating balance in relation to gravity - a deformed, unnatural posture develops.

This can easily be observed in older people who, for example, often walk bent forward due to such deformities. But this is not an inevitable fate. All you have to do is regularly prevent blockages of the energy flow in the 'three narrows'. This can be achieved, for example, through belly dance movements and meditation. This also makes you increasingly aware of your body and feelings, which in itself prevents blockages.

The pelvic floor, diaphragm and neck area of the body correspond spiritually with the subtle energy centres, which are called "chakra" in yoga. Thus, the pelvic floor corresponds to the root and sacral chakra, the diaphragm to the solar and heart chakra, the throat to the throat and forehead chakra and the spine to the crown chakra.

According to the popular view of yogis, the Kundalini, which rests in the root chakra, rises through the spine to the crown chakra and in this way leads to enlightenment (ecstasy). By regularly practising belly dance movements, we automatically stimulate the corresponding chakra in the energy body. Therefore, experiences of ecstasy can also occur through belly dancing. In any case, however, any physical blockage is dissolved again with regular practice and the dreaded body deformations and stiffness of old age do not occur.

Belly dance is, if you will, yoga in motion. The permanent movement in the corresponding parts of the body to the rhythm of the music relaxes the body and frees the mind from "obscurations". Performed regularly, it results in a lasting physical well-being. However, we must also be willing to engage with ourselves in order to free ourselves from blockages. We have to be open in the first place to perceive the unpleasant anxiety/pain associated with the blockages. For everything heavy must first be seen so that it can be transformed into lightness and relaxation.

If, due to the permanent isolated movement of individual body parts in the belly dance meditation, energy blockages want to come into consciousness with a time delay, this can express itself, for example, in states of anxiety or pain, or it can lead to panic attacks and nightmares.

First aid for such states as well as for black magic attacks, which express themselves in the same way, is offered from a shamanic point of view by laying hands on the painful spot as follows:

> Lie on the bed or on a blanket on the floor in the posture of the hanged man (Tarot), either on the back or on the stomach, whichever is more comfortable.

> Place the right hand on the painful part of the body (or on the heart if no painful part can be found, as in panic attacks and nightmares), the left hand on one the 8

centres and 4 corners of the body: crown, throat, shoulders, heart or diaphragm, navel, hips, pubic bone, tailbone, knees, soles of the feet; preferably on a spot as far away as possible from the painful part.

Then concentrate on the hands, including the place where the hands rest, and direct the breath. While doing this, breathe deeply into the heart and out into the hands. The thoughts are calmed by concentrating on the inhalation and exhalation. So think constantly of the hands and the part of the body they cover and breathe deeply in and out. This should gradually lead to calming down and the pain subsiding, allowing one to relax again, or, if the attack occurs at night, to fall asleep again. Usually the causes of the blockage appear in the dream afterwards.

If emotions arise with a time lag, allow them and surrender to them. *From experience, surges of emotion are short-lived, but they lead to the causes of the blockage.* (Cantieni) As soon as they have arrived in the consciousness, one is liberated. Afterwards, belly dance movements that were difficult at first suddenly come naturally and joy sets in.

Transformation in dance
In voodoo, elemental spirits take on supporting functions in the transformation of shadows through dance. Parallel to this, special forms of movement in belly dance also have corresponding effects on psychological problems and drive conflicts:
When we dance for ourselves, for example, the spirits of the air help with problems of happiness, contentment and our own state of mind. In this

case, dance mainly with the chest and upper body. Special exercises are shoulder shimmy, various movements of the shoulders, arms and hands, chest circles, pushing, lifting and lowering, body wave; veil dance. (6th and 7th chakra / mental body) - music recommendation: e.g. *Through the Ankh* by Hossam Ramzy

The wood spirits help with health problems (drive conflicts). Dance half circles, swing, tilt, pendulum, twist, push pelvis and hips; stick dance. (2nd chakra / causal body) - music recommendation: e.g. *Secrets of the Eye* by Hossam Ramzy

For money problems you can call upon the earth spirits with dances of stomping or sloshing such as drop steps, ¾ shimmy steps, hagalla, belly sloshing; cymbal dance. (4th chakra / etheric body) - music recommendation: e.g. *The Beauty of Your Eyes* by Hossam Ramzy.

For authority problems (lack of self-esteem), the water spirits help. For more self-worth and self-confidence dance circles, figure eights and waves; Baladi. (3rd and 5th chakra / astral body) - music recommendation: e.g. *Love is not Forbidden* by Hossam Ramzy

For problems with love and with spiritual existence in the broadest sense, the fire spirits help. Accordingly, we have to whirl, shake, twist, twitch and tremble to compensate, i.e. dance shimmys in all variations and turns; drum dance. (1st chakra / vital body) - music recommendation: e.g. *Never Mind* by Hossam Ramzy

Music is the key

Not all music is suitable for belly dance meditations. Music that corresponds to the dancer's 'mental rhythm' is important. Therefore, each dancer has to search herself for the music that is suitable for her. It is always music that really electrifies you, that gives you 'goose bumps', that makes you unable to sit still, that makes you have to dance. In this way, one overcomes the inner resistance ('demon'), the unwillingness, the inertia that wants to prevent one from freeing oneself from anxiety through the perception of personal balance.

In the belly is the 'second brain' or in other words: in the belly is the mounting point of the will / mind. However, belly dance meditation is an ancient method of restoring personal balance when the mounting point has shifted and the gap has appeared in the energy body through which death can occur. By becoming aware of the balancing force (Ma'at), the truth, the greater force of gravity, the gap is closed again, new balance is found and the life force is strengthened.

The energy body - the aura

Being a witch ...

...a shaman or a sorcerer means a certain view of the world and a certain attitude of mind. This world view, developed through long experience in dealing with nature and with the human psyche, together with the power of a pure heart and the observance of certain rules (e.g. celebrating the annual festivals, keeping the Book of Shadows, witch ethics[1], and so on), potentially enables the following abilities:

1. see into a possible future by means of oracle, crystal, black mirror, and so on
2. communicate with animals
3. casting spells or directing energies
4. have dialogues with nature and its spiritual beings
5. summoning elementals and light beings
6. contact with the underworld or otherworld
7. astral projections and lucid dreaming
8. working magically through inner strength with gesture, ritual, willpower and instinct
9. wandering between worlds (shamanic journeying)
10. healing / harming
11. cursing and breaking curses. Curses are mostly used as punishment. Unlike black magic manipulations, witchcraft curses manifest themselves by disappearing again without causing further harm when one expiates one's guilt.
12. to provide for the safety of the soul in this world and in the hereafter by means of the spirits
13. contact goddesses/gods and the deceased

Witches believe in the spiritual forces in nature and communicate with them by connecting with the personal nature spirit residing within themselves.

---

1   For example: If it doesn't harm anyone, do what you want.

In other words, they connect with their inner power, as part of the force of nature, in order to communicate with the rest of nature by means of it.

In order to connect with the inner power, they put themselves into an ecstatic state. Aids for this are e.g. dance, drum music, drugs. This kind of ecstasy cult was also known in antiquity and was still widespread among the people in the Middle Ages and was demonised, persecuted and fought against by the church from the middle of the 14th century. *In the 'dark' Middle Ages, communication is not limited to people. Communication was with plants, animals, spirits, demons, the dead, saints, martyrs, God and Goddess, among others. "The world is completely ensouled and enchanted."* (Schwanitz, Die Geschichte Europas)
Even today, in some areas of Greece, the former land of the goddesses Aphrodite and Artemis, the spring festival of Anthestaria is still celebrated ecstatically with the entire community, with church approval and under ecclesiastical auspices (feast of St. Constantine), during which people dance for three days and finally walk over burning coals in an ecstatic state without burning their feet.
The return of the life force to nature was celebrated ecstatically in this way in spring and taken over into one's own life to strengthen one's own soul force.
The world view from antiquity continued in the Middle Ages (1000 years after all). In addition, since the collapse of the Roman Empire with the migration of peoples, the ecstasy cults of the nomadic tribes that had migrated from Asia continued to spread throughout Europe and increasingly competed with the worldview of the

rising power of the Christian Church, which strictly denied a paradise on this side in harmony with nature and denigrated what was natural in man as sin.

Since the beginning of the modern era and the development from a feudal to a monetary economy, the rejection by the church was additionally accompanied by the political will of the secular authorities to be able to "... *shape all areas of human existence 'rationally', according to coldly calculable rules ...*". (Golowin, Die weisen Frauen)

This is how it has remained until today. A one-sided emphasis on the rational led to technical progress on the one hand, but also to the spiritual impoverishment of modern man on the other.
In our degenerated society without a spiritual connection to nature, the destruction of nature through technical progress, e.g. by means of artificial intelligence, has taken on huge proportions and inevitably led to the downfall of the entire human race. For, if one makes oneself dependent on AI, one completely betrays one's own divine nature and becomes a plaything of the environment, a slave to the dead things outside. Thereby one also becomes a dead thing.
However, we did not come into the world to let ourselves be determined and reified by others, but to balance our destiny and to perfect ourselves in our humanity. This is only possible through the further development of our consciousness in the sense of expanding the boundaries of consciousness into the irrational or, to put it another way, shifting the boundaries of perception into the supersensible.

The art of the witch therefore consists in balancing both realms, the rational (tonal) and the irrational (nagual). The boundary between these two realms is the fence on which the witch sits.

Appendix

The magical year - permanent calendar

Days with a special vibration

On these days it is much easier to achieve ego
transcendence through dance, to contact one's own
spirit and build up the energy needed to cast
spells. Dance:

- Veil dance for an insight spell with incense
  - 1/15 Jan., 24 Jun., 23 Aug., 31 Oct., 1/22
  Nov.

- Stick dance for a healing spell with herbal
  magic - 26 Feb., 17/25 March, 15/19 Apr., 6
  May, 1/21 Jun., 19 Jul., 15 Aug., 28 Sept.,
  21 Dec.

- Cymbal dance for a wealth spell with gemstone
  or amulet consecration - 16 Feb., 21 March,
  19/30 Apr., 1/6/18/24 May, 9 Jun., 19 Jul.,
  28 Sept., 26 Oct., 16 Nov., 21/31 Dec.

- Baladi for invoking the Goddess and for a
  full moon ritual - 6 Jan., 1/2/16 Feb., 14
  Jun., 1/15 Aug., 21 Sept., 11 Oct., 1/25 Dec.

- Drum dance for a transformation with candle
  magic - 30 Jan., 14 Feb., 1 March, 15/30
  Apr., 1/18 May, 3/19 Jul., 13 Sept.

MARCH - SPRING - increasing Yang

1	Feast of Juno
2	
3	
4	
5	Feast of Isis
6	
7	
8	
9	
10	
11	
12	
13	
14	Feast of Snake goddess
15	

MARCH - SPRING - increasing Yang

16	
17	Feast of Libera
18	
19	
20	
21	Feast of Ostara - Spring equinox
22	
23	Feast of Bastet
24	
25	Feast of Mati
26	
27	
28	
29	
30	
31	

Days with a special vibration in March:

1 March - Feast of the goddess Juno,
Protective goddess of married women. Good day to
make amulets, lucky charms, talismans, to undergo a
ritual cleansing of the house / flat and to create
a pleasant atmosphere with incense sticks or aroma
lamps.
5 March - Festival of Isis
Ancient Egyptian goddess of magic. Daughter of the
sky goddess Nut and the earth god Geb. Similar to
the Greek goddess Demeter, she is a guardian of the
family and the earth circle.
14 March - Festival of the snake goddess Ua Zit or
Nagini.
Food or drink offerings are made to the snake
goddess and prayers are made for the expulsion of
poverty.
17 March - Festival of the goddess Libera
Roman goddess of agriculture and nature. Good day
to gather herbs and make tinctures, prepare sweets
and offer some of your sweetmeats to the goddess.
21 March - Festival of the goddess Ostara or Tara
Spring equinox. Good day to hold fertility and
wealth rituals. Be sure to go outside today and
feel and absorb the energies.
23 March - Festival of the Goddess Bastet
Ancient Egyptian goddess of the hunt. As the "eye
of Re" she destroys his enemy Apophis. The goddess
Diana corresponds to her among the Romans and the
goddess Artemis among the Greeks.
25 March - Festival of the goddess Mati
Goddess of the earth. Good day for sowing and also
for asking the goddess' protection for the plants.
Afterwards, make a libation to the goddess.

APRIL- SPRING - increasing Yang

1	
2	
3	
4	
5	
6	
7	
8	
9	
10	
11	
12	
13	
14	
15	Feast of Tellus Mater

APRIL- SPRING - increasing Yang

16	
17	
18	
19	Feast of Ceres
20	
21	
22	
23	
24	
25	
26	
27	
28	
29	
30	Walpurgis Night

Days with special vibration in April/May:

15 April - Feast of the Goddess Tellus Mater.
Roman earth mother goddess. Good day for love
spells, renewing life force, gathering and
processing herbs.

19 April - Feast of the goddess Ceres
Roman earth mother goddess. Bad day for travelling
and gathering medicinal herbs. Good day for candle
magic, light purification, rituals with incense,
fire sacrifices to ask protection for plants.

30 April - Walpurgis Night
The night of 1 May is suitable for witch dancing,
drumming, rattling, casting spells for love.

1 May - Beltane - Witch Festival
Good day for fertility / wealth rituals.

6 May - Festival of the Goddess Inghean-Bhidhe
Irish goddess of the beginning of summer. Good day
to plant a rowan tree, nurture it and ask the
goddess for health and prosperity.

18 May - Feast of the god Pan
Greek god of love and every witch's dream man. If
you dance for Pan, you can meet your dream man in
your dreams. Ideal day for love, money transactions
and rituals with candle magic.

24 May - Festival of the goddess Kali
Indian goddess, wife of the god Shiva. She is a
goddess of transformation and rebirth. The name
Kali means 'the black one'. She is said to have
once come to southern France in May and is still
worshipped there by Roma tribes as 'Sara la kali'.
Kali is a strong goddess of protection and defeats
all demons. Good day for protection and banishing
rituals.

MAY - SPRING - Yang

1	Beltane
2	
3	
4	
5	
6	Feast of Inghean-Bhidhe
7	
8	
9	
10	
11	
12	
13	
14	
15	

MAY - SPRING - Yang

16	
17	
18	Feast of Pan
19	
20	
21	
22	
23	
24	Feast of Kali
25	
26	
27	
28	
29	
30	
31	

Days with a special vibration in June:

1 June - Festival of the Goddess Carna.
Roman goddess of nutrition. Cook a dish and offer
part of it to the goddess. Good day for meditation.
9 June - Feast of the goddess Vesta
Roman goddess of the hearth. Good day to restore
the blessing of the house by making a fire offering
to the goddess.
14 June - Birthday of the Muses
Nine Greek goddesses, daughters of Zeus. They
inspire art and culture. Good day for a candle
ritual to inspire a project in this area.
21 June - Summer Solstice
Celebrate outside around a bonfire today, remember
the transience of all that exists and be grateful
for your own life. Collect elderflowers, prepare a
tea and drink it to strengthen your vitality.
24 June - St. John's Day, Day of the Goddess of
Fortune, Day of the Fairies
Perhaps a fairy will meet you today and grant you a
wish. Perhaps you will have good luck.

JUNE - SUMMER - increasing Yin

1	Feast of Carna
2	
3	
4	
5	
6	
7	
8	
9	Feast of Vesta
10	
11	
12	
13	
14	Birthday of the Muses
15	

JUNE - SUMMER - increasing Yin

16	
17	
18	
19	
20	
21	Litha - Summer Solstice
22	
23	
24	St. John's Day, Feast of Fortuna, Day of the Fairies
25	
26	
27	
28	
29	
30	

JULY - SUMMER - increasing Yin

1	
2	
3	Feast of Cerridwen
4	
5	
6	
7	
8	
9	
10	
11	
12	
13	
14	
15	

JULY - SUMMER - increasing Yin

16	
17	
18	
19	Marriage of Isis and Osiris
20	
21	
22	
23	
24	
25	
26	
27	
28	
29	
30	
31	

Days with special vibration in July / August:

3 July - Festival of the Goddess Cerridwen.
Celtic goddess of transformation and rebirth. Good
day for fertility rituals of all kinds. Give thanks
to the goddess with a libation.
19 July - Marriage of Isis and Osiris
Ancient Egyptian deities. Isis was worshipped even
in Germany by the Sueven tribe. She is also
considered the goddess of magic: Isis makes
everything whole again!
Osiris is considered the god of the underworld, the
'guardian of the threshold'.
Good day for spells of all kinds.
1 August - Lammas
Celtic harvest festival. Gratitude for the gifts of
nature and life are appropriate today. Respect and
reverence for the forces that shape and sustain
life.
13 August - Feast of Hecate
Greek goddess of the underworld. She is invoked
mainly at new moon to banish harm that might affect
the harvest.
15 August - Assumption of Mary
Patroness of women. Day of the consecration of
herbs. Weave a wreath of herbs, hang it on the
outside of the house and ask Mary for protection
from all 'evil'.
23 August - Feast of the Moirs
Three Greek goddesses of fate. Good day to ask the
goddesses to help with the 'inner martial arts' of
dealing with one's own character.

AUGUST - SUMMER - increasing Yin

1	Lammas
2	
3	
4	
5	
6	
7	
8	
9	
10	
11	
12	
13	Feast of Hekate
14	
15	Assumption of Mary

AUGUST - SUMMER - increasing Yin

16	
17	
18	
19	
20	
21	
22	
23	Feast of the Moirs
24	
25	
26	
27	
28	
29	
30	
31	

Days with a special vibration in September:

13 September - Festival of the Goddess Venus.
Roman goddess of love, comparable to Aphrodite.
Good day for love spells of all kinds.
19 September - Festival of the god Thoth
Ancient Egyptian god of wisdom and magic. He helps
us to keep the two realms of Tonal (rationality)
and Nagual (irrationality) in balance.
21 September - Autumnal equinox.
Celtic Mabon Festival. Today, the spiritual forces
of nature are thanked for their guidance and help
in casting spells. The magical utensils are
cleansed and recharged with new energy.
28 September - Festival of the Goddess Baubo
Greek goddess of laughter. Reminds us not to take
ourselves too seriously and not to take everyday
life with its constraints too seriously, but to
look at it with humour. Laughter is healthy.

SEPTEMBER - AUTUMN - increasing Yin

1	
2	
3	
4	
5	
6	
7	
8	
9	
10	
11	
12	
13	Feast of Venus
14	
15	

SEPTEMBER - AUTUMN - increasing Yin

16	
17	
18	
19	Feast of Thot
20	
21	Mabon - Autumn Equinox
22	
23	
24	
25	
26	
27	
28	Feast of Baubo
29	
30	

OCTOBER- AUTUMN - increasing Yin

1	
2	
3	
4	
5	
6	
7	
8	
9	
10	
11	Feast of Demeter
12	
13	
14	
15	

OCTOBER- AUTUMN - increasing Yin

16	
17	
18	
19	
20	
21	
22	
23	
24	
25	
26	Feast of Hathor
27	
28	
29	
30	
31	Night on Samhain

Days with a special vibration in October:

11 October - Feast of the Goddess Demeter.
Greek goddess of agriculture as well as goddess of
state, marriage, household, child care. Offerings
from forests and fields are made to the goddess
Demeter and prayers are made for justice and peace
for all mankind.
26 October - Feast of the goddess Hathor
Ancient Egyptian goddess of love, beauty and fate,
art and culture, also ruler of the underworld.
Hathor's law is the metamorphosis of opposites into
their opposite, as depicted in the Great Arcanum of
the Tarot. I Ching is also a book of change. Both
oracles provide information about the workings of
the forces of destiny.
31 October - Samhain
On the night of Samhain the borders between the
worlds are opened. Use the night for contact with
deceased friends and family members in dreams, if
you wish to do so.

NOVEMBER - AUTUMN - Yin

1	Samhain
2	
3	
4	
5	
6	
7	
8	
9	
10	
11	
12	
13	
14	
15	

Days with a special vibration in November:

1 November - Samhain
Celtic holiday. Beginning of the new witch year.
The old year is evaluated retrospectively. The gods
are thanked for benevolence and support. Oracles
are consulted to part the veil between the worlds,
to see into the future and to become clear about
oneself.
16 November - Night of Hecate
Greek goddess of the moon. Hecate helps witches to
strengthen their own power by offering her a food
or drink sacrifice at a crossroads at midnight.
22 November - Feast of the goddess Artemis
Goddess of the hunt. Good day to perform rituals
for self-confidence.
*"Inner peace begins the moment you decide not to
allow events or other people to control your
emotions."* (Pema Chödrön)

NOVEMBER - AUTUMN - Yin

16	Night of Hekate
17	
18	
19	
20	
21	
22	Feast of Artemis (egypt. Bastet)
23	
24	
25	
26	
27	
28	
29	
30	

Days with a special vibration in December:

1 December - Feast of the Goddess Bona Dea.
Roman goddess of fertility and gynaecology. A good
day to celebrate a festival with friends where
protective amulets are made together and dedicated
to the goddess.
21 December - Winter solstice, festival of the
goddess Lucina, a Roman goddess of light; Yule.
The rebirth of the sun is celebrated. Decorate the
home with candles and celebrate the return of life
force to nature.
25 December - Feast of the goddess Holle.
Germanic weather goddess and goddess of the
underworld. She rewards industrious people and
gives a home to the souls of deceased children.
31 December - second festival of the goddess Vesta
Good day to greet the future together with loved
ones.

DECEMBER - WINTER - increasing Yang

1	Feast of Bona Dea
2	
3	
4	
5	
6	
7	
8	
9	
10	
11	
12	
13	
14	
15	

Days with special vibration in January / February:
1 January - Festival of the Goddess Nanshe.
A good day to consult oracles.
6 January - Feast of the triune moon goddess Luna.
Protect your home magically against theft, burglary and
cheaters by cleaning the outside of the apartment/house
door with vinegar water and writing the letters C, M, B
(Catherina, Margareta, Barbara) on it with your index
finger, thus consecrating your home to the moon goddess.
15 January - Feast of the goddess Carmenta
Patron goddess of midwives and expectant mothers. Good
day for divination, looking into the future (after
ritual purification).
30 January - Festival of the goddess Pax
This goddess of peace gives us the occasion to settle
old feuds and to consider how family life can be made
more harmonious. Flower decorations and candles create a
good mood.
1 February - Feast of the goddess Birgit.
Goddess of poetry and healing. Her symbol is the magic
cauldron and fire is subject to her.
A good day to commemorate her with candles and to make
healing ointments.
2 February - Candlemas
Good day for candle magic and amulet making to protect
against lightning and fire.
14 February - Valentine's Day / Lupercalia
You can make love amulets and celebrate an erotic feast
with your beloved. In ancient Rome, people celebrated
Lupercalia, a festival of fertility for the animal herd,
forest and fields.
16 February - Feast of Hecate
Goddess of sorcery and the underworld. Good day for
incantations, rituals with incense, fire sacrifices and
candle magic.
26 February - Feast of Hygeia
Goddess of health and hygiene. Good day to take good
care of oneself, to pamper oneself, to start a therapy
or to let the soul 'dangle'.

16	
17	
18	
19	
20	
21	Jul – Feast of Lucina
22	
23	
24	
25	Feast of goddess Holle
26	
27	
28	
29	
30	
31	Second Feast of Vesta

JANUARY - WINTER - increasing Yang

1	Feast of Nanshe
2	
3	
4	
5	
6	Feast of Luna (chr.: Holy Three Kings)
7	
8	Feast of Justitia (egypt. Ma'at)
9	
10	
11	
12	
13	
14	
15	Feast of Carmenta

JANUARY - WINTER - increasing Yang

16	
17	
18	
19	
20	
21	
22	
23	
24	
25	
26	
27	
28	
29	
30	Feast of Pax
31	

FEBRUARY - WINTER - increasing Yang

1	Imbolc – Feast of Birgit
2	Candlemas
3	
4	
5	
6	
7	
8	
9	
10	
11	
12	Feast of Diana (egypt. Bastet)
13	
14	Rome: Lupercalia (chr. Valentine's Day)
15	

16	Second Feast of Hecate
17	
18	
19	
20	
21	Rome: Feralia / Festival to appease the spirits of the dead
22	
23	
24	
25	
26	Feast of Hygeia
27	
28	
29	

Literature

Mikhael Bulgakov, Der Meister und Margarita
Paul Busson, Die Auferstehung des Melchior Dronte
Benita Cantieni, Tiger-Feeling
Carlos Castaneda, Das Feuer von Innen
Edgar Cayce, Über Sexualität und Erleuchtung
Daniel Dufour, Das verlassene Kind
Michael Harner, Der Weg des Schamanen
Ulrike Hegers, Bauchtanz
Oskar Hodosi, Licht-Tantra
Erik Hornung, Geist der Pharaonenzeit
Richard L. Johnson, Ich schreibe mir die Seele frei
Serge Kahili King, Der Stadtschamane
Maria Langwasser, Hexenwissen alt & neu
Shakti Morgane, Die Lichtwesen des Tarot
Shakti Morgane, Die Richtung der Kraft
Shakti Morgane, Kalender der Göttin
Shakti Morgane, Orientalischer Tanz und Ekstase
Arno Plack, Die Gesellschaft und das Böse
Heinz-Peter Röhr, Wege aus der Abhängigkeit
Samuel Sagan, Rückführung – free of charge at
clairvision.org
Shalila Sharamon, Bodo Baginski, Das Chakra
Handbuch
José Silva, Robert B. Stone, Der Silva Mind
Schlüssel zum inneren Helfer
Lillian Too, Feng Shui Lebensplaner
Tenzin Wangyal Rinpoche, Übung der Nacht
Richard Webster, Schütze Dich!
Claudia von Werlhof, Die Verkehrung
Eva Wlodarek, Weil du es dir wert bist
Kareen Zebroff, Yoga für Jeden

The author studied Russian Studies at the FU Berlin, Germany. She wrote her master's thesis on the occult, on the significance of the hidden reality in M. Bulgakov's novel: The Master and Margarita. Inspired in this way, Far Eastern and Oriental philosophies and religions, as well as Taoism and the ancient Egyptian religion, also helped her in her search for the meaning of life behind the hidden connections of reality.

Yoga, meditation, oriental dance and other eastern exercises for body and mind also expanded consciousness and acted as an aid in solving problems and finding orientation in everyday life.

Today, as a follower of the 'Ancient Path', she is a member of FOI, a community for the worship of the Goddess.